A Casebook on Contract

Flori   Roman

A Casebook on Contract

Second Edition

ANDREW BURROWS

MA, BCL, LLM (Harvard), QC (Hon), FBA, Honorary Bencher of Middle Temple, Norton Rose Professor of Commercial Law in the University of Oxford and a Fellow of St Hugh's College

·HART·
PUBLISHING

OXFORD AND PORTLAND, OREGON
2009

Published in North America (US and Canada) by
Hart Publishing
c/o International Specialized Book Services
920 NE 58th Avenue, Suite 300
Portland, OR 97213-3786
USA
Tel: +1 503 287 3093 or toll-free: (1) 800 944 6190
Fax: +1 503 280 8832
Email: orders@isbs.com
Website: www.isbs.com

Hart Publishing, 16C Worcester Place, Oxford, OX1 2JW
Tel: +44 (0)1865 517530 Fax: +44 (0) 1865 510710
Email: mail@hartpub.co.uk
Website: http://www.hartpub.co.uk

British Library Cataloguing in Publication Data
Data Available

ISBN: 978-1-84113-993-7

Typeset by Forewords, Oxford
Printed and bound in Great Britain by
TJ International Ltd, Padstow, Cornwall

IN MEMORY OF MY FATHER

Acknowledgements

The author and publisher gratefully acknowledge the authors and publishers of extracted material which appears in this book, and in particular the following for permission to reprint from the sources indicated:

Justis and the Incorporated Council of Law Reporting for England and Wales—the Law Reports, the Weekly Law Reports and the Industrial Cases Reports.

LexisNexis Butterworths—extracts from the All England Law Reports, the All England Reports Commercial Cases, Family Court Reports and Law Times Reports.

Informa UK Ltd—extracts from Lloyd's Law Reports and Building Law Reports.

Sweet & Maxwell Ltd (Westlaw)—for an extract from the Fleet Street Reports and an extract from Commercial Law Cases.

While every care has been taken to establish and acknowledge copyright, and to contact copyright owners, the publishers apologise for any accidental infringement and would be pleased to come to a suitable agreement with the rightful copyright owners in each case.

Preface

In my view, the best way for students to understand and enjoy the law of contract is by careful analysis of what the judges have said in the leading cases. It is with that in mind that I have written this book. It aims to make the cases readily accessible through a clear structure, by a succinct introductory commentary to the various sections, and by notes and questions that will enable a student to appreciate the significance of a particular case and the interesting issues raised by it. Novel features include the treatment of statutes, where I have tried to give a principled overview of the central provisions, and the summaries of academic writings either as part of the notes on a particular case or in the additional reading at the end of each chapter. Above all it is hoped that the book will convey the fascination and excitement of this central subject.

This is a casebook in the traditional sense that it is designed to be used alongside, rather than as a replacement for, a textbook. There are several excellent textbooks on contract. I have given references throughout to the three that I consider the best. As an introductory book, most usefully read at the start of a topic, I would recommend Ewan McKendrick, *Contract Law*. If the student is going to buy any other books I would recommend, as a more detailed textbook, Jack Beatson, *Anson's Law of Contract* and, as a more theoretical work, Stephen Smith, *Atiyah's Introduction to the Law of Contract*. But obviously teachers and students have their own favourites and this casebook can be used just as easily with any other textbook.

This book is aimed at all those studying contract, in particular undergraduates on law courses. The contents seek to reflect the scope of most modern university courses so that the law on illegality and incapacity is not included.

Three further particular features of the contents should be noted. The first is the prominence given to remedies. Both theoretically and in practice this topic is, arguably, the most important in contract law and yet often it is pushed to the end of a course where it is not given the attention it merits. It is to be found in the centre of this book as Part Three. The second is the recognition of the interplay between contract law and the drafting of contract terms. Lawyers need a detailed knowledge of contract law not only to advise when things go wrong but also in order to be able to draft contracts effectively. Proper attention is therefore paid at various stages of this book to interpretation and to various types of contract term. The third is the use made of the outstanding comparative work of the Commission on European Contract Law (led by Olé Lando and Hugh Beale). Their *Principles of European Contract Law* (PECL) merits greater attention by students than has traditionally been the case. What I have done here, therefore, is to set out the relevant parts of PECL at the ends of chapters (along with the page references to the detailed commentary) so that students can compare PECL with English law once they have mastered a particular topic. My own square-bracketed comments are then designed to help a student to see, and to think about, the differences. I have chosen PECL rather than the equally impressive Unidroit Principles of International Commercial Contracts because, given the ongoing talk of a European Contract Code, they are, arguably, of greater importance.

The extracts from the statutes are reproduced in the most recent form with all amendments being incorporated within square brackets.

By the time a student has worked his or her way through this book, he or she will have favourite judges who can be relied on for rational and clear exposition of contractual principles. I anticipate that most will derive the greatest illumination from the judgments of Lord Denning, Lord Wilberforce, Lord Steyn, Lord Nicholls and Lord Bingham. It is striking how much more sophisticated judicial reasoning on contract has become albeit that this coincides with ever longer judgments.

There are several people I would like to thank. Hugh Collins who, along with the late great Peter Birks, taught me contract at Brasenose College and is the author of a deservedly popular theoretical text, *The Law of Contract* (4th edn, 2004); Lyn Hambridge for her secretarial skills; my excellent research assistants for the first edition, Andrew Scott (who helped with Chapter 4), Adam Rushworth (who assisted with Chapters 11–13) and Kira King (who helped on Chapters 14–15); and Richard Hart, Mel Hamill and Tom Adams at Hart Publishing for being such a great pleasure to work with and for being so encouraging and efficient from start to finish.

New cases covered in this second edition include: *Adam Opel GmbH v Mitras Automotive (UK) Ltd*; *Collier v P & M J Wright (Holdings) Ltd*; *Lymington Marina Ltd v Macnamara*; *Balmoral Group Ltd v Borealis (UK) Ltd*; *Abbey National Plc v Office of Fair Trading*; *Golden Strait Corp v Nippon Yusen Kubishika Kaisha, The Golden Victory*; *Transfield Shipping Inc v Mercator Shipping Inc, The Achilleas*; *Statoil ASA v Louis Dreyfus Energy Services, The Harriette N*; *Edwinton Commercial Corporation v Tsavliris Russ (Worldwide Salvage & Towage) Ltd, The Sea Angel*; and *CTI Group Inc v Transclear SA, The Mary Nour*. New articles referred to include those by Tettenborn, Robertson, Rotherham, Pearce and Halson, and McLauchlan.

This edition is again dedicated to my father who died from cancer as I was nearing completion of the first edition. If I can be half as good a father to my four children as he was to me, I will have done a wonderful job.

Andrew Burrows
28 February 2009